ST. THOMAS AND HISTORICITY

The Aquinas Lecture, 1979

ST. THOMAS
AND HISTORICITY

Under the auspices of the
Wisconsin-Alpha Chapter of Phi Sigma Tau

By
ARMAND MAURER, C.S.B.

MARQUETTE UNIVERSITY PRESS
MILWAUKEE
1979

Library of Congress Catalog Number 79-84278

© Copyright 1979
Marquette University

ISBN 0-87462-144-5

Dedicated to the memory of
PAUL M. BYRNE
Professor of Philosophy
Marquette Universiy

Prefatory

The Wisconsin-Alpha Chapter of Phi Sigma Tau, the National Honor Society for Philosophy at Marquette University, each year invites a scholar to deliver a lecture in honor of St. Thomas Aquinas.

The 1979 Aquinas Lecture *St. Thomas and Historicity* was delivered in Todd Wehr Chemistry on Sunday, February 25, 1979, by the Reverend Armand Maurer, C.S.B., Professor of Philosophy at the Pontifical Institute of Mediaeval Studies and at the University of Toronto.

Fr. Maurer was born in Rochester, New York, in 1915. He was ordained a priest in the Congregation of St. Basil in 1945. His graduate work was done at the Pontifical Institute of Mediaeval Studies and the University of Toronto, from which he holds a Ph. D. He has done post-doctoral work at the University of Paris and at Harvard University. In 1954 he received a Guggenheim Fellowship for the study of medieval philosophy. He was elected to the Royal Society of Canada in 1966.

The focus of Fr. Maurer's research has been on the philosophies of the thirteenth and fourteenth centuries. His translation and study of Aquinas' *On Being and Essence* appeared in 1949. He published *St. Thomas Aquinas: The Division and Methods of the Sciences. Questions V and VII of his Commentary on the De Trinitate of Boethius* in 1953 and *Meister Eckhart: Parisian Questions and Prologues* in 1974. Fr. Maurer has written articles that have appeared in *Mediaeval Studies, The New Scholasticism, Speculum,* and *The Encyclopedia of Philosophy.* In the Random House *A History of Philosophy* Fr. Maurer is the author of the second volume, *Medieval Philosophy.* Along with Thomas Langan and Etienne Gilson, Fr. Maurer wrote the fourth volume, *Recent Philosophy: Hegel to the Present,* to which he has contributed the parts on English and American Philosophy.

To Fr. Maurer's distinguished list of publications, Phi Sigma Tau is pleased to add *St. Thomas and Historicity.*

St. Thomas and Historicity

I am pleased and honored to be invited
to give the Marquette Aquinas Lecture of
1979. For many years I have watched the
series of small red volumes of Aquinas Lectures grow on my bookshelf. Little did I
think that one day I would be asked to add
to their number.

As the volumes appeared year after year
I read them with interest and profit, but
there was one that especially set me thinking. I am referring to Emil Fackenheim's
Lecture of 1961 on "Metaphysics and Historicity".[1] Some of you no doubt heard the
Lecture and many of you, like myself, have
read it in its printed form; and I think you
will agree with me that it was memorable
for its profound assessment of the predicament in which metaphysics finds itself today. As Fackenheim sees it, this predicament can be summarized as follows. Since
the middle of the nineteenth century meta-

physicians have questioned the capacity of the human mind to reach truths transcending time and history. They have denied that the philosopher can rise above history and grasp timeless truths. Plato and Aristotle, Aquinas and Avicenna, Descartes, Kant and Hegel certainly disagreed in what the truths of metaphysics are, but they shared the conviction that metaphysical truths are valid for all men and for all time.

Nietzsche opened the way to a revolution of metaphysics by asserting the death of God and at the same stroke historicizing metaphysical truth. Truth, for Nietzsche, is the will-to-power, and since this will changes from age to age and culture to culture, it no longer transcends history but is essentially tied to it. In the wake of Nietzsche a long line of philosophers have historicized metaphysical truths, among them Collingwood, Dilthey, Croce, Dewey and Heidegger.

Closely linked with this revolutionary view of metaphysical truth is a new conception of man. His very being, like his

truth, is now viewed as completely historical. Contrary to the older view of man as
possessing a permanent nature underlying
his historical and cultural changes, the
more recent philosophy of man refuses
him a fixed and abiding nature. Nothing
essential or substantial to man remains
throughout his history. The being itself of
man is inseparable from his history, just
like the grasp of his metaphysical truth.
As metaphysical truth differs from one
period of history to another, so too does
the being of man. Again, just as metaphysical truth is a product of man's self-willing
and self-making, so too man's being is a
self-making or self-constituting process. In
this perspective, Fackenheim writes, "Man
is not endowed with a permanent nature
capable of acting. His 'nature' is itself the
product of his acting, and hence not a
proper nature at all. *In acting, man makes
or constitutes himself.*"[2] So metaphysics
and human nature are in the same situation: both are forms of self-making. Radically historical and temporal, they admit
of no transhistorical or timeless features.

This in a nutshell is Emil Fackenheim's description of the situation of metaphysics today as a consequence of the doctrine of historicity. Why is he so concerned about it? What predicament does it lead to? Why does it bother him as a metaphysician? The reason is this: If metaphysics does not rise above history and reach transhistorical and stable truths, then all metaphysics is reduced to a sequence of historically relative world views (*Weltanschauungen*). Metaphysics in principle is superseded by history. There is a history of metaphysics, but beyond this history there is no room for an independent inquiry into metaphysical truth. In short, historicity of metaphysics leads to historicism; and historicism is vitiated by an intrinsic contradiction. For, while insisting on the changing and relative character of all metaphysical truths, it wishes to exempt at least one of them from this condition, namely the thesis on which historicism is based: that the mind changes through history because it is its own self-constituting activity. All acts of human self-making are historically situated, with the one exception of the act by which self-making recognizes itself as self-making and as historically situated. Thus historicism finds itself in the self-contradictory situation of denying that there are any transhistorical truths, and affirming a transhistorical truth as the basis of the doctrine[3].

In his Aquinas Lecture Fackenheim does not presume to solve the problem raised for the contemporary metaphysician by the doctrine of historicity. His main concern is to state the problem, and this he does clearly and profoundly. At the end of the lecture he wonders whether we should not abandon the whole doctrine of human self-making and return to what he calls "the classical doctrine of a human nature" in order to escape the inconsistency of historicism. And he invites those who hold for a human nature to dialogue with him on the subject. Since he was giving an Aquinas lecture no doubt he was addressing his invitation above all to Thomists. He asks whether the classical doctrine of a human nature has the resources to meet

the contemporary existentialist objections
against it. Can this doctrine assimilate the
insights into selfhood and self-making
achieved from Kant to Heidegger without
collapsing in the process? These questions,
he assures us, "invite what might well become the most profound metaphysical dialogue in our time."[4]

A few years after giving his lecture I
met Emil Fackenheim on the Toronto
campus and he expressed his disappoint-
ment with the small reaction it had pro-
voked. Since then, the theme of historicity
and metaphysics has been taken up on
various occasions, for example at the meet-
ing of the American Catholic Philosophical
Association in 1969 and again in 1974.[5] But
without denying the value of these dis-
cussions, I think there is still a place for a
dialogue with Professor Fackenheim, and
I would like to use this occasion to begin
it. In the first part of this lecture I would
suggest that the historicity of man and
human self-making are compatible with a
notion of human nature, though not with
every notion of human nature, and cer-

tainly not with the one we have inherited from the rationalism of the nineteenth century. In the second part I would propose that historicity is consistent with the transcendence of truth, though not with every notion of truth, and clearly not with the notion of eternal truths that has come down to us from late scholasticism and early modern philosophy. To be more specific, I would contend that the Thomistic doctrines of man and truth are capable of admitting the positive values of the philosophies of historicity while avoiding their inconsistency.

1. Human Nature and Self-Making

Let us begin the dialogue by considering the notion of human nature. Fackenheim wonders if "the classical doctrine of human nature" is incompatible with the historicity of man and self-making.[6] But is there one classical notion of human nature? Plato, Aristotle, Thomas Aquinas, Descartes, Kant—these among other philosophers professed doctrines of human nature,

but no two are identical. If any two might
be thought to share a common notion of
man they would be Aristotle and St.
Thomas. Are they not responsible for what
is generally known as the scholastic notion
of man as a rational animal, endowed with
a permanent substantial essence, which is
capable of accidental modifications but of
no essential change or development? And
was it not exactly this concept of human
nature as "a reality ready-made prior to
the self's own acting, and yet fully human"
that Fichte and others have rejected as
both metaphysically and morally intol-
erable?[7]

And yet, historians have shown beyond
all doubt that Aristotle and Aquinas did
not share a common doctrine of human
nature, that even their notions of nature
were profoundly different. Aristotle conceived nature (*physis*) as an inner principle of physical bodies determining them
to act in definite, specific ways towards
determinate ends.[8] Because of its nature
earth moves to the center of the world;
plants and animals grow and develop with

an inner necessity of nature to be specific-
ally different living things. Though Aristotle sometimes used the term "nature"
more broadly to designate any kind of
being, he preferred to limit it to physical
bodies, for they alone exhibit growth and
change, which are implied in one of the
basic meanings of the word *physis*.[9]

The Aristotelian notion of nature was
appropriated by Aquinas, but he broad-
ened and deepened it to become a prop-
erly analogous concept expressing the
intelligible essence of a being—a concept
that is realized in essentially different ways
in physical bodies, plants, animals, men,
angels and God.[10] In St. Thomas' vocabu-
lary there is not only corporeal nature, but
also sensitive nature, rational nature, intellectual nature, even divine nature. Aristotelian nature, as form or actual entity,
tended to be fixed and determined in itself
and in its causality. Thomist nature, on the
level of spiritual creatures, is a principle
both of specification and of freedom and
transcendence, even of openness to a supernatural perfection and destiny.

St. Thomas' Christian conception of
nature is closely linked to his new notion
of being (*esse*) as the act of existing. For
Aristotle, nature in the sense of form was
the highest actuality.[11] In the new metaphysics of St. Thomas the act of existing
is the supreme actuality and perfection.[12]
Nature, in the created order, is only a possibility of existing; to exist, it has to be
actualized by existence. In this new perspective human nature is an openness to
existence and to all the nature's existential
possibilities.

This transformation of the notion of
nature, prepared no doubt by Christian,
Jewish and Muslim philosophers of the
Middle Ages, but accomplished by St.
Thomas, would have been impossible without the revealed doctrine of creation. As
the handiwork of God, nature is open to
his influence. Man is a special case of nature for he has been created in the image
of God, and this image is found in his intellectual nature.[13] And as the image of
God he is by his nature drawn to his cre-
ator: *fertur, vel nata est ferri in Deum.*[14]

He is not by nature closed in upon himself; he is open to the infinite riches of God. As Karl Jaspers says, man is not "simply one living species among others; he discovers himself as something unique, embracing everything, open to everything."[15] Karl Rahner expresses the same view when he writes that of its very nature spirit possesses a limitless transcendence, which gives the human horizon an infinite character.[16]

In this connection Rahner criticizes what he calls the "scholastic concept" of nature as applied to man. He asks whether this concept is not too closely modelled upon nature that is less than human:

What is signified by the 'definition' and hence the circumscription of man's 'nature', if he is the essence of transcendence, and hence of the surpassing of limitation? Is it meaningful at all in such a perspective simply to assign to this 'nature' an end perfectly defined materially? Not as though the remotest doubt were being thrown here on the fact that man has a nature and that this in itself has an end assigned to it. But these must not and cannot be conceived in such simple terms as the mutual order of a pot and its lid or of a biological organism and its fixed environment. One has only to ask why a supernatural end can be set for man without annulling his nature, and why God cannot do this with the nature of something below man.[17]

Rahner concludes that only in a highly analogous way can the notions of nature and end be extended to the various grades of being, and especially to man.

Henri de Lubac agrees with Rahner on this point, though he thinks the scholastic concept of human nature criticized by Rahner, "which borrows too much from the sub-human," is not that of Thomas Aquinas but of modern scholasticism. De Lubac points out that Aquinas habitually distinguishes between natural things (*res naturales, naturalia*) and human things and human nature (*res humanae, natura humana*). A natural thing is limited and contained in being, whereas human nature has greater fullness and breadth (*habet maiorem amplitudinem et extensionem*).[18] A first indication of this is the mind's capacity to become other things by receiving their forms in knowledge. These forms enrich and develop the being of the knower beyond his limited natural being, to the point that the perfection of the whole universe can exist in him.[19] He can also open himself to others, drawn to them by love. A spirit incarnate in a body, he is not just an individual, separated from other individuals; he is a person, destined to fulfill himself by communion with other persons of his own time and of the past. Thus his spiritual nature is the ground of his sociability and also of his historicity.[20] His full destiny, however, does not lie in these natural modes of enrichment and communion, but in the face to face vision of God, which he can achieve not by his own natural resources but by grace.[21]

In the perspective of St. Thomas, man's openness to the full range of being, and even to infinity, through his reason is the ground of his freedom.[22] Man, in short, is free precisely because he has a rational nature. We should notice that for Aquinas freedom is not opposed to nature, as it is in the philosophy of Kant. Kant conceived nature as a closed system, utterly determined by law.[23] It makes no sense in his view to speak of man as free by nature; but it does make good sense to Thomas Aquinas. It is understandable that philosophers who inherited the Kantian notion of nature should have rejected a human nature as incompatible with human freedom. For them, the exaltation of human freedom must result in the denial of a human nature. Free self-determining and self-making cannot be grounded in human nature, as they are in the thought of Thomas Aquinas. Nothing could point up more forcefully the gulf between the Thomistic notion of nature and that of Kant and the post-Kantians. Etienne Gilson once wrote that Thomistic nature is not Aristotelian nature.[24] We might add, neither is it Kantian nature.

Because man is free, he is able to choose this or that, make up his mind, select his own course of action. And his choice bears not only upon his will and deeds, but more importantly upon himself. By making up his mind, in a true sense he makes himself. Freedom means nothing if not *self*-deter-

mination and *self*-making. Karol Cardinal
Wojtyla (the future Pope John Paul II)
put this well in his address to the Thomistic
Congress of 1974 in Rome and Naples:

> . . . self-determination is the manifesta-
> tion of the fact that not only the active
> directing of the subject towards a value
> takes place in the act of the will. There
> is more in it: there is man, who in this
> act turns towards a definite value and
> thus decides not only about this move,
> but by making it he also decides about
> himself. The concept of self-determina-
> tion contains more than the concept of
> agency: man not only performs his ac-
> tions, but by his actions he becomes, in
> one way or another, his own 'maker'.[25]

One way in which he does *not* make himself is to give himself his substantial essence or nature. The Cardinal went on to
say that from the very beginning a person
is "somebody" in the metaphysical sense.
But he insisted that a man by his free de-
cisions throughout life becomes more and
more "somebody" in the personal and
moral sense. By acquiring moral, intellectual and artistic qualities he makes himself

more fully a person and a more perfect human being.[26]

Because he has a mind, the human person not only "makes" himself in these and other ways, but he also creates his own social, technological and cultural worlds. In this he differs from all other animals. Thomas Aquinas observes that nature is not lacking in providing the necessities of life. To subhuman animals nature provides suitable weapons and covering: teeth, claws, nails, fur, shell, etc. But nature acts differently in the case of man: it gives him reason and hands by which he can provide these things for himself. He is left free to arm and clothe himself as he wishes.[27] Thus reason is at once the ground of man's freedom and the source of his self-enrichment not only through knowledge and love, but also through art and technology.

There is then a wide gulf between the world of physical nature or things and the human person. As Anton Pegis liked to remind us, man is a spirit incarnated in a body. Because the human spirit is by nature the form of the body, it is engaged in time and history, and this precisely in order to become fully human and thus achieve its destiny. Pegis wrote:

> The human soul, which is a spiritual substance *as* the form of matter, is an intellectual creature destined by nature for a historical existence, for an incarnate and therefore temporal duration, in order to express and to realize the intellectuality proper to it.[28]

But what is human nature if it can transcend itself in this way? What is this mysterious center within us that gives us the capacity of free self-determination and self-development? St. Thomas never doubted that we have a permanent nature or essence that specifies us as *human* beings, but he was equally convinced that we do not know this nature in itself. The essences of things are unknown to us (*rerum essentiae sunt nobis ignotae*),[29] and St. Thomas makes no exception of the human essence. We define man as a rational animal, and this definition satisfies the demands of logic, that a definition should give the proximate genus and spe-

cific difference of what is defined. But this
definition hides, as much as it reveals, the
real essence of man. We say the specific
difference of man is rationality, but this
is a property of his nature and not his *substantial* difference. In place of man's essential difference from other animals, St.
Thomas says, we use his power of reason-
ing or his having a mind. Because this
power flows from his essence, it can designate it and in a way disclose it, as an effect
can make known its cause.[30]

If this is true, we have no a priori knowledge or direct intuition of human nature
that would tell us what it means to be
fully human. We come to know his potentialities by observing the works of the
human mind: language, science, art, religion, history, myth. These Ernst Cassirer
calls "the defining and determining circle
of humanity";[31] but it is not a closed circle.
We are constantly in amazement of what
man can achieve, for good or for ill, and
as we observe his achievements we grow
in our understanding of his nature.[32]

Of course, no one would deny that man

has limitations. Even the devotees of historicity grant that man always acts within
a given situation, either natural, historical
or human, and that this situation imposes
limits upon him. The notion of man as a
self-constituting process must be compatible with the fact that I cannot make myself to be a lion, or live in the year 700
A.D., or lift three tons by my own strength.
So we need not deny man a human nature
on the ground that it would impose limitations on him. We should only refuse him
a nature if it were inconsistent with his
capacity for self-making and self-transcendence. It is clear that a material nature,
like a stone or even a subhuman animal,
would be incapable of the sort of self-
making we observe in man.[33] But because
man is rational, there is no incompatibility
between his having a nature and his transcending his being. For man's rationality
and freedom are not something fixed and
closed, given to him ready-made at the
beginning of his life. He is always in the
process of developing them, as he is forever building his world.

Let me hasten to add that the notion
of self-making is not found in the works
of St. Thomas. Like the concept of historicity, it has emerged in our own time,
which is more historically-minded and
self-reflective than his. But far from op-
posing the notion, his philosophy seems to
invite it, and it finds its place in a living
Thomism.

2. Historicity and Transcendence of Truth

So far we have been considering the
possibility of reconciling man's self-making
with his possessing a human nature. I have
tried to show that there is no contradiction between them in the Thomist perspective. It is time to turn to our second problem and ask: Is the doctrine of historicity
compatible with the transcendence of
truth, or does it inevitably involve historicism?

Once again Emil Fackenheim can help
us to see the problem clearly. Six years
after his Aquinas Lecture, in 1967, he
addressed the seventh Inter-American

Congress of Philosophy on the subject "The Historicity and Transcendence of Philosophic Truth."[34] This paper is a further development of one aspect of his earlier Aquinas Lecture. That lecture centered around the theme of self-making and human nature; the subsequent lecture turns more directly to the question of historicity and philosophic truth. Fackenheim is not concerned with a truth such as "I am speaking these words now," which will not be true in a moment, but with philosophic truths.[35] Are they also so bound up with specific historical situations that they can claim no transcendence or universality? If they can make no such claim, all philosophy would be historical and there could be no rational argument between philosophers of different ages or cultures.

We have already seen Fackenheim refuse this historicism, and his refusal is well founded. In the very act of historicizing their truth, philosophers engage in rational argument with thinkers of the past and of different cultures. It appears that philosophy cannot do without transcendent and

universal truths. But does this mean that
we have to revert to the notion of eternal
truths enshrined in the *philosophia perennis?* In Fackenheim's words (which
have a clear echo of Plato), must we escape
"from the cave of history into a realm of
eternity"? And if we take refuge in the
timeless, eternal truths of perennial philosophy, do we not have to abandon the
historicity of philosophic truth?[36]

Clearly Fackenheim is unhappy about
eternal truths in philosophy. Like Heidegger, he is not comfortable with them;[37] but
once they have been eliminated, does not
historicity permeate philosophic truth so
thoroughly as to destroy every vestige of
transcendence, with disastrous consequen-
ces for philosophy?

As an alternative to the historicism of
the later Heidegger and to the timeless,
eternal truths of perennial philosophy,
Fackenheim wonders if there may not be
universal, transcendent philosophic truths
which are grounded in history and arise
from history. Such truths would have the
mark of history upon them, but they would

still be universal and transcendent. It is possible, he suggests, that the "loss of an eternal realm of truth may not necessarily mean the loss of all universal truth." And this leads him to formulate his central problem: *"How can philosophic thought be rooted in history, and emerge from history, and yet reach a truth which is transcendent?"*[38] He feels that if an answer to this question can be found we shall have saved both the historicity of philosophic truth and its universality and transcendence. At the same time we shall have avoided the notion of eternal truths, free of all historical taint and independent of the world of experience, proposed by the *philosophia perennis.*

At this point let us begin our dialogue with Fackenheim again and ask: What is the *philosophia perennis* of which he speaks—the tradition which claims to reach timeless, eternal truths uncontaminated by the world of experience and history?[39] Is Thomism a part of this tradition?

The doctrine of eternal truths was a commonplace among the late scholastics

and early modern rationalists. Scotus, Vas-
quez and Suarez vigorously defended the
eternal verities, and they occupy an im-
portant place in the systems of Descartes,
Malebranche, Spinoza and Leibniz. The
relation of these truths to the divine mind
was warmly debated. Descartes contended
that they were eternally established by
God as the supreme legislator.[40] Since they
depend on the divine will, God could have
created mathematical and metaphysical
truths otherwise than he did. For example,
he could have made it untrue that the three
angles of a triangle be equal to two right
angles. Leibniz disagreed: in his view the
divine understanding gives reality to the
eternal truths without the intervention of
the divine will, and so they are not changeable.[41] Neither Descartes nor Leibniz went
as far as some Scotists, who boldly claimed
that even if God did not exist, the eternal
truths would still be true.[42]

Throughout this debate the eternal
truths were given a status of their own. Pure
and uncontaminated by time, they hovered
between the human mind and God—ghosts

as it were of the Platonic Ideas.[43] Duns
Scotus played a large role in shaping this
notion of the eternal truths, for he assigned
to them a "diminished" being and eternity,
formally distinct from the divine mind.[44]
Under the influence of Scotus, Suarez described the eternal truths as a grand spec-
tacle, distinct from God and contemplated
and enjoyed by him. Propositions expressing them, he says, "have eternal truth not
only as they exist in the divine mind, but
also in themselves, abstracting from that
mind."[45] He realized that on this point he
was deviating from St. Thomas, for he
knew that St. Thomas "refers the whole
eternity of truth to the divine mind."[46] But
if Aquinas is correct, he asks, how can the
eternal truth of necessary propositions be
safeguarded? How can we meet the objection of "modern theologians" who claim
that propositions about creatures are not
eternally true, but begin to be true when
things come to be and lose their truth
when things perish? It is hardly enough
to reply with St. Thomas that when creatures cease to exist these propositions are

true, not in themselves, but in the mind of
God, for in this sense even contingent
truths exist eternally in the divine mind.[47]
Necessary truths, like those of mathematics and metaphysics, must accordingly
have an eternity of their own, prescinding
from the mind of God.

If we turn to the works of St. Thomas,
we see that Suarez' world of eternal truths
is conspicuously absent. St. Thomas' con-
stant teaching is that there are not many
eternal truths; there is only one, and that
is the truth of the divine mind. This follows from the fact that truth is being, and
the conformity of mind to being. Hence
anything is related to truth as it is related
to being: *unumquodque . . . ita se habet
ad veritatem sicut ad esse.*[48] Now only the
divine being and mind are eternal. The
conclusion is inevitable: only the divine
truth is eternal; and since there is only
one divine mind, there is only one eternal
truth.[49]

The truth of the human mind, on the
contrary, is not eternal but temporal. St.
Thomas leaves us in no doubt on the mat-

ter: "Because our mind is not eternal,
neither is the truth of propositions which
are formed by us eternal, but it had a beginning in time."[50] Do we not experience
the birth of truth in us when we learn or
discover it? We make up our mind, form a
true judgment, and thereby we make its
truth, and we do this in time.[51] St. Thomas
never loses sight of the fact that the human
mind in itself, as a spiritual substance,
transcends time,[52] but he insists that because it is incarnated in a body it is subject
to time and change. Our thoughts and af-
fections succeed one another in time.[53] We
know one thing before and another after.
We remember the past, see the present and
anticipate the future. God's knowledge, on
the contrary, is free from change and temporal succession. In him there is no past
or future: everything is eternally present
to his sight.[54]

Human truth, then, is not eternal, and
neither is it unchangeable. Once again St.
Thomas is explicit: "The truth of the divine
mind is unchangeable, but the truth of our
mind is changeable."[55] He does not mean

that a truth, say of metaphysics or mathematics, is subject to change, but that the truth of our intellect is. Our mind, in short, is not unchangeably true. For truth exists in a mind: it is the known conformity of mind to being, and this conformity, like any relation, varies with the change in the terms of the relation. If the object of our mind does not change, but our judgment about it does, our judgment becomes false. If we assert that Socrates sits while he sits, our assertion is true. But if we change our judgment to "Socrates stands" while he still sits, our judgment becomes false. If Socrates should stand and we continue to judge that he sits, our judgment becomes false. In order to remain true, we must change our judgment to "Socrates rises." Thus the truth of our judgment can become false, or change to another truth, with the change of our judgment or its object.[56]

In some cases our judgment cannot change and remain true as long as its object exists. This is always so when it is a question of the essential properties of things.

As long as men exist, it is true that they are rational, for rationality is of the essence of man.[57] But if all men ceased to exist, we would say men *were* rational. Now that dinosaurs no longer inhabit the earth, we say they *were* animals. Thus our understanding of things changes with the change of time: *secundum variationem temporis sunt diversi intellectus.*[58]

The truth of the human mind, then, is not completely unchangeable, and neither is it necessary. "In creatures," St. Thomas says, "there is no necessary truth."[59] At first sight this is a surprising statement, for are there not in the mind of the mathematician and metaphysician necessary truths, i.e. truths that cannot be otherwise? St. Thomas does not deny this, or that (as we shall see) the mind can think about these truths just in themselves, quite apart from their existence in any mind. What he is denying is that any truth exists necessarily in a created mind. There is no necessity that our mind be conformed to being, or that once it has achieved this conformity it maintain it.

Nothing shows better than this St. Thomas' existential view of truth. Truth is completed, he says, by an act of the mind, and it has for its foundation the being (*esse*) of things.[60] So we must judge of truth as we judge of the mind and being. Now there is only one mind and being that is eternal, completely immutable and necessary, namely the divine. Hence St. Thomas' conclusion: truth in the human mind is not eternal, completely immutable or necessary.

The obvious objection, which St. Thomas does not fail to raise, is that truths like "Every whole is greater than its part" seem to be immutable and necessary. In reply, he concedes that there are necessary propositions, but he insists that they are not necessarily true *in our mind*. The truth of these propositions *per accidens* can lose its existence in the human mind and in things, if they should cease to exist. In this case, these truths would remain only in God, in whom they would be one and the same truth.[61]

The same existential approach to truth

inspires St. Thomas' answer to the objection that there is an eternal created truth, for according to St. Augustine there is nothing more eternal than the nature of a circle, and that two and three are five. Surely these are created truths and nevertheless eternal! St. Thomas' reply is curt: "The nature of a circle, and the fact that two and three make five, have eternity in the mind of God."[62]

Human truth, then, is not to be confused with divine truth. Like human being itself, human truth is at once temporal and historical. Aquinas has often been criticized for presenting a static and anti-historical system of theology and philosophy. The German historian Alois Dempf claims that history meant nothing to Aquinas, nor had he any need of it. Moving in a supra-temporal sphere, he saw only the supra-temporal side of truth and recognized no need of progress in the sciences.[63] These harsh judgments of Thomism echo the statement of Nietzsche, that Aquinas and his work are situated outside of history, so to speak "six thousand feet beyond men and time,"[64] and Hegel's opinion that in the Middle Ages truth "remains a heavenly truth alone, a Beyond."[65]

I trust by now these illusions have been dispelled. St. Thomas in fact was well aware of the role of history in human thought.[66] With Aristotle, he recognized time as a kind of discoverer or good partner in the progress to truth. Not that time itself contributes anything, St. Thomas hastens to add, but help comes with time. An inquirer into truth will understand later what he did not see before, and learning of his predecessors' discoveries he will be able to go beyond them. The arts grow in a similar way. Someone will make a small discovery, and this will gradually lead to great ones.[67]

St. Thomas' own practice reveals his sense of history and of his indebtedness to it. He not infrequently marks out the stages in the discovery of a truth, as when he traces the progress of philosophers in understanding the nature of being. These men, he comments, "little by little, and as it were step by step, advanced in the knowledge of the truth."[68] Everything of value that he found in these philosophers he appropriated in his own doctrine, and then he advanced beyond them with his original insights. As a theologian he followed the same practice of making his own the tradition of the Fathers and medieval masters, then adding his own contribution to the understanding of the faith.

For Aquinas, then, truth does not descend from the blue; it is achieved in time and through history. It always has the mark of history upon it, for it lives and develops in a mind that is historically situated. Moreover, in its linguistic expression it always carries the signature of a special language, different from other idioms in which it may be formulated.[69]

This satisfies one of Fackenheim's requirements, that philosophic truths be rooted in the temporal world and emerge from history. What can be said about his other stipulation, that the truths of philosophy be universal and transcendent? This is also met, for although the mind is incarnated in the body, unlike material

forms it is not wholly immersed in matter.
As a spiritual substance it keeps its transcendence over matter and time. The best
proof of this is its ability to abstract natures
from spatial and temporal conditions.[70]
We can form universal concepts and make
universal judgments about the things we
experience which are true always and
everywhere. Such, for example, is the judgment that men are rational. We can then
give formal expression to these universal
truths in propositions and think about them
just in themselves, or absolutely, abstracting from the existence they have in a
mind.[71] We can focus our attention on
them, without considering whether they
exist temporally in us or eternally in God.
We can do the same thing with a nature
or essence when we think of it just in itself,
or absolutely, without considering whether
it exists as a universal in the mind or as an
individual in reality. When philosophic
truths are considered in this way they are
necessary and indestructible, as an essence
absolutely considered is necessary and immutable. The mind in which they exist

changes by learning or forgetting them, but in themselves they are not subject to change. Truths considered absolutely can even be called "eternal", not in the positive sense that they enjoy an eternal being, but in the negative sense that they abstract from change and time.[72]

Because truths can be considered absolutely or in themselves, it is tempting to think that they have a kind of entity in themselves, distinct from the being of the mind in which they exist. A similar illusion is at the basis of the notion that an essence in itself has its own essential being (*esse essentiae*) quite apart from the existence (*esse existentiae*) it has in the real world. There were Platonizing philosophers in the Middle Ages, like Henry of Ghent and Duns Scotus, who fell prey to this illusion.[73] When they turned their attention to necessary truths, they also endowed them with an intelligible or "diminished" being and eternity, distinct from the full being and eternity of God. Thus was born the scholastic notion of eternal truths that was to bedevil modern rationalism. Heidegger recognized them for what they are: "residues of Christian theology within philosophical problematics," and he called for their complete elimination.[74] But the theology from which they came was not that of Thomas Aquinas. If there is a perennial tradition of eternal truths, Thomism is not part of it. Aquinas never doubted the existence of an eternal truth which is at once the origin and goal of human truth, but this eternal truth is the divine Truth, and it is one, as God himself is one.

But does the loss of eternal truths compel us to abandon the transcendence of philosophic truth? Must we remain in the cave of history until the day we enjoy the vision of eternal Truth? Not at all. For the human mind, a spirit in its own right, can reach universal truths that transcend the limits of time and matter, while falling short of eternity. If this is so, we are not left with the two horns of Fackenheim's dilemma: either historicism or eternal truths in philosophy. There is a way out, and he himself has shown it to us in words that, I believe, Thomas Aquinas would accept: ". . . philosophic thought seeks radical universality, and the truths to which it lays claim transcend history even if they encompass, not eternity but merely all time or all history."[75]

Conclusion

At the beginning of this lecture I raised two related questions: Is human nature compatible with self-making? and: Is transcendence of truth reconcilable with its historicity? I have tried to show that both questions can be answered in the affirmative with the philosophy of St. Thomas, provided that it is understood authentically and not confused with later scholasticism. It is vital in this connection to see the difference between St. Thomas' existentialist approach to man and truth and the essentialist views of the later scholastics, who were the vehicles by which scholasticism came to be known by modern philosophers. I hope I have convinced you—provided of course you really needed convincing!—that Thomism is not part of a classical or perennial tradition defined

in terms of this later scholasticism. Perhaps
I have also persuaded you—provided you
needed to be persuaded!—that St. Thomas'
views on man and truth leave Thomism
open to all that is valuable in the new ap-
proaches to self-making and historicity,
while giving them a solid metaphysical
foundation.

I am under no illusion, however, that
even if St. Thomas' philosophy were recognized for what it is, it would be readily
accepted by our contemporaries. For is
not its starting point the very one explicitly
rejected by most modern philosophers, that
is to say the reality of the external world?
In cognition, St. Thomas gives the primacy
to the external; only secondarily, by way
of reflection, does thinking take cognizance
of itself and become its own object.[76] With
Descartes, modern philosophy took a new
subjective turn, shifting primacy in knowledge from things to consciousness or thinking. The "Copernican revolution" was
already begun, and the whole of Western
civilization was henceforth to bear its im-
print.

But this revolutionary turn in philosophy was to bring with it new problems, at least as serious as those it was designed to avoid. For if the philosopher must begin philosophizing with consciousness or thought, how can he ever reach anything transcending it? Is he not forever enclosed within thought, as the idealists contend? The problem of the openness of thinking to what is other than thinking becomes acute indeed. Along with this problem of transcendence goes the problem of universality. For where can I begin philosophizing about thought and its ideas except with my own; and from there how can I reach a thought that is common to myself and others, especially those of different times, cultures and languages? In Hegelian terms, how can my finite thought overcome its limitations and be sublated in a transcendent, universal thought?

These problems, which are endemic to transcendental philosophy from Fichte, through Hegel, to the contemporary phenomenologists, do not arise for St. Thomas, because in his view cognition from the outset opens upon a meaningful world beyond cognition. The objectivity of perception and thought at once transcends knowledge and contacts a world that is not simply *my* world, made meaningful by *me*, but one whose intelligibility reveals itself to the mind and which we can share with others. Indeed, the intellect by its very nature is pointed to the universal: our first conception is being, which is the most universal of all notions. It is true that being as initially conceived is the being of sensible things, but it contains an intelligible light that allows the mind to mount to a Being that is subsistent and eternal.

Does not the crisis of metaphysics and historicity described so well by Fackenheim result from the transcendental turn taken by philosophy since Descartes? If so, there is no easy solution to the crisis. It calls for a radical counter-Copernican revolution in which it will no longer be assumed that objects must conform to our knowledge, but that knowledge must conform to things.[77]

NOTES

1. (Milwaukee: Marquette University Press, 1961).
2. Ibid., p. 26 (author's emphasis).
3. Ibid., p. 63. In a later paper Fackenheim considers his "formal-dialectical refutation" of historicism inadequate, pointing out that Heidegger himself (whose historicism Fackenheim is chiefly concerned with) already anticipated it. See E. Fackenheim, "The Historicity and Transcendence of Philosophic Truth," *Proceedings of the Seventh Inter-American Congress of Philosophy* (Québec: Les Presses de l'Université Laval, 1967), I, p. 79. It is not enough to dispose of historicism by charging it with self-contradiction, but it must be inquired whether, and if so how, the world of experience, which is historical, can provide a ground for universal and transcendent truth (p. 86). My concern in the present lecture is not whether Heidegger was successful in surmounting his historicism, but how St. Thomas Aquinas accounts for universal and necessary philosophic truths drawn from a changing world by temporally situated humans.

Of course a philosopher can escape the self-contradiction described by Fackenheim by claiming that all knowledge is historically and culturally conditioned, even the doctrine of historicity. But then he must abandon every claim to grasp universal and permanent truths. He must be content to speak to his own time and culture and have nothing to say to mankind. Few, if any, great philosophers, novelists, dramatists or poets would so limit themselves. As Fackenheim says of the arts: "any single work of genius is a living witness testifying that the total historization of the arts is absurd." *Metaphysics and Historicity*, p. 66.

4. Ibid., p. 99.

5. *Truth and the Historicity of Man, Proceedings of the American Catholic Philosophical Association*, 43 (1969). The Presidential Address was given by W. Norris Clarke, "On Facing up to the Truth about Human Truth." The Presidential Address in 1974 was given by Thomas D. Langan on "Historicity and Metaphysics." See *Proceedings of the American Catholic Philosophical Association*, 48 (1974), pp. 1-13. See also L. B. Geiger, "Métaphysique et Relativité Historique," *Revue de Métaphysique et de Morale*, 60 (1952), pp. 381-414; A. Dondeyne, "L'Historicité dans la Philosophie Contemporaine," *Revue Philosophique de Louvain*, 54 (1956), pp. 5-25; 456-477. Same author, *Foi Chrétienne et Pensée Contemporaine* (Louvain: Publications Universitaires, 1952), pp. 11-52.

6. Ibid., p. 98.

7. Ibid., p. 95.

8. For Aristotle's notion of nature, see A. Mansion, *Introduction à la Physique Aristotélienne*, 2nd ed. (Louvain-Paris: Editions de l'Institut Superieur de Philosophie, 1946), pp. 80-105. J. Owens, *The Doctrine of Being in the Aristotelian Metaphysics*, 3d ed. (Toronto: Pontifical Institute of Mediaeval Studies, 1978), p. 190.

9. See Aristotle, *Metaph.*, V, 3, 1014b16-1015a19. "Aristotle himself lists meanings of 'nature' signifying a permanent principle, and acknowledges that by extension it may designate any kind of being; but in his own usage he prefers to re-

strict it to the sensible order." J. Owens, *A History of Ancient Western Philosophy* (New York: Appleton-Century-Crofts, 1959), p. 309. ". . . 'nature' (*physis*) means for Aristotle the powers and functions of natural bodies." J. H. Randall, *Aristotle* (New York: Columbia University Press, 1960), p. 173.

According to Aristotle, mind "can have no nature of its own, other than that of having a certain capacity [to become all things]." *De Anima*, III, 4, 429a22. See *De Partibus Animalium*, I, 1, 641b9.

10. For St. Thomas' notion of nature, see *Summa Theologiae*, III, q. 2, a. 1. The Aristotelian notion of nature is here developed in the context of Christology.

11. See J. Owens, *The Doctrine of Being in the Aristotelian Metaphysics*, pp. 185, 458. "The distinctive character of a truly Artistotelian metaphysics of being . . . lies in the fact that it knows of no act superior to the form, not even existence." E. Gilson, *Being and Some Philosophers*, 2nd ed. (Toronto: Pontifical Institute of Mediaeval Studies, 1952), p. 47.

12. ". . . hoc quod dico esse est inter omnia perfectissimum. . . . Quaelibet autem forma signata non intelligitur in actu nisi per hoc quod esse ponitur. Nam humanitas vel igneitas potest considerari ut in potentia materiae existens, vel ut in virtute agentis, aut etiam ut in intellectu: sed hoc quod habet esse, efficitur actu existens. Unde patet quod hoc quod dico esse est actualitas omnium actuum, et propter hoc est perfectio omnium perfectionum." *De Potentia Dei*, q. 7, a. 2, ad 9m (Rome: Marietti, 1942). See *Summa Theol.*, I, q. 4, a. 1, ad 3m.

13. See St. Thomas, *Summa Theol.*, I, q. 93, a. 4, 6. See L. B. Geiger, "L'homme, Image de Dieu. A Propos de 'Summa Theologiae' I, 93, 4," *Rivista di Filosofia Neo-Scholastica*, 46 (1974), pp. 511-532.

14. "Et sic imago attenditur in anima secundum quod fertur, vel nata est ferri in Deum." *Summa Theol.*, I, q. 93, a. 8.

15. K. Jaspers, *Bilans et Perspectives* (Paris: 1945), p. 159. Cited by H. de Lubac, *The Mystery of the Supernatural*, trans. R. Sheed (New York: Herder & Herder, 1967), p. 138.

16. See K. Rahner, *Mission and Grace*, trans. C. Hastings (London: Sheed & Ward, 1963), I, p. 127. The infinity of the human spirit, for St. Thomas, is not absolute but relative (*secundum quid*), i.e. with respect to knowledge. Absolutely speaking the mind is finite ("intellectus noster simpliciter finitus est," *Summa Contra Gentiles*, I, 69, n. 14). See J. H. Robb, *Man as Infinite Spirit* (Milwaukee: Marquette University Press, 1974). For Hegel, man has both finite and infinite aspects, but his finitude is sublated in the infinity of Spirit. See E. Fackenheim, *Historicity and Metaphysics*, p. 69. See the remarks of J. Maritain, *Moral Philosophy* (New York: Scribner's, 1964), p. 149.

17. K. Rahner, *Theological Investigations*, trans. C. Ernst (Baltimore: Helican Press, 1961), I, p. 317. Cited by H. de Lubac, ibid., p. 139.

18. St. Thomas, *Summa Theol.*, I, q. 14, a. 1.

19. ". . . et ideo in III De Anima dicitur, 'animam esse quodam modo omnia' quia nata est omnia cognoscere; et secundum hunc modum possibile est ut in una re totius universi perfectio existat."

De Veritate, q. 2, a. 2; ed. Leonine (Rome, 1970), 22, p. 44.

20. "Parce qui'il n'est pas un pur esprit, mais un esprit qui s'anime dans la matière, l'homme n'est présent à lui-même qu'en sortant de soi. Il ne se voit dans sa réalité intérieure qu'en se tournant vers le monde des objets et des hommes. Il n'est personne que lorsqu'il est avec une autre personne; la conscience de soi est la conscience d'un soi-dans-le-monde, une conscience d'être avec les autres hommes. Ainsi la structure métaphysique de l'homme comporte une ouverture radicale à l'histoire et une dépendence de l'histoire." M.D. Chenu, "Création et Histoire," *St. Thomas Aquinas 1274-1974. Commemorative Studies.* (Toronto: Pontifical Institute of Mediaeval Studies, 1974), II, p. 394.

21. "Unde haec est ultima perfectio ad quam anima potest pervenire secundum philosophos ut in ea describatur totus ordo universi, et causarum eius, in quo etiam finem ultimum hominis posuerunt, qui secundum nos erit in visione Dei, . . ." *De Veritate*, q. 2, a. 2; ed. Leonine, p. 44. *Expositio super Librum Boethii de Trinitate*, q. 6, a. 4, ad 5m; ed. B. Decker (Leiden: E. J. Brill, 1955), p. 229.

22. ". . . radix libertatis est voluntas sicut subiectum; sed sicut causa, est ratio . . ." *Summa Theol.*, I-II, q. 17, a. I, ad 2m. See ibid., I, q. 83, a. 1.

23. "By nature, in the empirical sense, we understand the connection of appearances as regards their existence according to necessary rules, that is, according to laws." Kant, *Critique of Pure Reason*, trans. N. K. Smith (London: Macmillan, 1950), A 216, B 263; p. 237. "This independ-

ence of the mechanism of nature is 'freedom in the strictest sense' or transcendental freedom." L. W. Beck, *A Commentary on Kant's Critique of Practical Reason* (Chicago: University of Chicago Press, 1960), p. 179.

24. E. Gilson, *Le Philosophe et la Théologie* (Paris: Fayard, 1960), p. 60. "An Aristotelian nature is fixed, determined and self-enclosed in its finality. How can a free spirit, called by God to receive the gift of Himself, be explained as an Aristotelian nature?" A. C. Pegis, "Man as Nature and Spirit," *Doctor Communis,* 4 (1951), p. 61.

25. K. Wojtyla, "The Structure of Self-Determination as the Core of the Theory of the Person," *Atti del Congresso Internazionale. Tommaso d'Aquino nel suo Settimo Centenario,* 7 (Naples: Edizioni Domenicane Italiane, 1978), pp. 40-41.

Kierkegaard wrote: "Therefore, while nature is created out of nothing, while I myself as immediate personality am created out of nothing, as a free spirit I am born out of the principle of contradiction, or born by the fact that I choose myself." *Either/Or,* trans. Lowrie (Princeton: Princeton University Press, 1944), II, p. 179. Cited by E. Fackenheim, ibid., p. 85, note.

26. "Man not only decides about his actions, but he also decides about himself in terms of his most essential quality. Self-determination thus has as its corresponding counterpart the becoming of man as such (the consequence of this is that he becomes more and more 'somebody' in the personal and ethical sense, though in the metaphysical sense he has from the beginning been somebody . . .)." K. Wojtyla, ibid., p. 41.

This human development takes place by acquiring intellectual and moral virtues, which in

St. Thomas' language, are "accidents" of the human substance. These "accidents," however, are not superficial or unimportant additions to the substance; on the contrary, they profoundly affect the human being. One has only to remember that, for St. Thomas, supernatural grace is an "accident" to realize how deeply an "accident" can transform the human person.

27. See St. Thomas, *Summa Theol.*, I-II, q. 5, a. 5, ad 1m.

28. A. C. Pegis, *At the Origins of the Thomistic Notion of Man* (New York: MacMillan, 1963), p. 52. "What is man? A free projection in history, much like a comet burning its way across the heavens? Assuredly he is, and he has exercised the genius of many artists who have sought to capture him, if not in his essence, at least in his passage. With St. Thomas we are aware, in a way that is unique to him, that if man is a historical sort of being, indeed the only being in the universe that is historical by nature, this trait belongs to the soul before it belongs to man. History is the signature of the soul's intellectuality, for the human soul is an intelligence living by motion at the level of the intelligibility found in matter. That is why it is a man, a temporal spirit, engaged in an incarnated intellectual life." *Ibid.*, pp. 46-47.

29. "Quia vero rerum essentiae sunt nobis ignotae, virtutes autem earum innotescunt nobis per actus, utimur frequenter nominibus virtutum vel potentiarum ad essentias designandas." St. Thomas, *De Veritate*, q. 10, a. 1, pp. 296-7. See ibid., q. 4, a. 1, ad 8m, p. 121; *In VII Metaph.*, lect. 12 (Rome: Marietti, 1950), n. 1552. In some cases the properties and accidents of a

thing observed by the senses sufficiently disclose its nature: *sufficienter exprimunt naturam rei.* See *In De Trinitate Boethii*, q. 6, a. 2; ed. B. Decker (Leiden: E. J. Brill, 1955), p. 216, lin. 2. In the context, St. Thomas means that the observable data sometimes are adequate to constitute a science of nature. On this point see J. Maritain, *The Degrees of Knowledge*, trans. G. B. Phelan (London: Geoffrey Bles, 1959), pp. 176-177, 204-207.

30. ". . . quia substantiales rerum differentiae sunt nobis ignotae, loco earum interdum diffinientes accidentalibus utuntur secundum quod ipsa accidentia designant vel notificant essentiam ut proprii effectus notificant causam; unde sensibile, secundum quod est differentia constitutiva animalis, non sumitur a sensu prout nominat potentiam sed prout nominat ipsam animae essentiam a qua talis potentia fluit; et similiter est de rationali vel de eo quod est habens mentem." St. Thomas, *De Veritate*, q. 10, a. 1, ad 6m, p. 299.

31. Cassirer, in the wake of Kant, rejects a definition of man in terms of an "inherent principle which constitutes his metaphysical essence," or "by any inborn faculty or instinct that may be ascertained by empirical observation." He allows only a functional, not a substantial definition of man's nature. See E. Cassirer, *An Essay on Man* (New Haven and London: Yale University Press, 1944), pp. 67-68. For the Thomist, the functional unity Cassirer finds in the activities and works of man are grounded in his substantial unity, more precisely in the unity of his being (*esse*).

32. Dilthey's assertion, quoted by E. Fackenheim,

Metaphysics and Historicity, p. 13, n. 9: "only history brings to light the potentiality of human being *(Dasein)*" is an overstatement; other disciplines besides history can reveal the powers of man.

Have man's essential potentialities long been disclosed? (see ibid., p. 14). They would be fully disclosed only if we had an exhaustive knowledge of man's essence, which, according to St. Thomas, is beyond us. In fact, we have only a general knowledge of human potentialities, as we have of his nature. One can agree that "If there is a human nature, then the historical changes of human self-understanding are as irrelevant to that nature as are the changes in the physical sciences to physical nature." But this does not mean that human *being* is not historically situated or that human understanding (including self-understanding) does not affect human being. Human nature or essence, for the Thomist, is not equivalent to human *being*. The Thomist does not reduce being to essence.

33. The impulse or tendency towards self-transcendence is already found in nature below man in its evolution towards higher forms. See J. Maritain, "Vers une Idée Thomiste de l'Evolution," *Approches sans Entraves* (Paris: Fayard, 1973), pp. 105-162.

34. See above, note 3.

35. Ibid., p. 77.

36. Ibid., pp. 79-80.

37. "Both the contention that there are 'eternal truths' and the jumbling together of Dasein's phenomenally grounded ideality with an idealized absolute subject, belong to those residues of Christian theology within philosophical prob-

lematics which have not as yet been radically extruded." Heidegger, *Being and Time*, I, 6, 229; trans. J. Macquarrie & E. Robinson (New York & Evanston: Harper & Row, 1962), p. 272.

38. E. Fackenheim, ibid., p. 82 (author's emphasis).

39. The notion of perennial philosophy goes back to the Renaissance, when Augustinus Steuchus used the term to mean a consensus of religious piety among all philosophers, culminating in the Christian religion. See his *De Perenni Philosophia* (Basel, 1542), X, 1, p. 649. Leibniz revived the term to mean a continuous philosophic tradition going back to antiquity. See Leibniz, *Lettre III à Rémond; Opera Omnia*, ed. J. E. Erdmann, I, 704a. But, as J. Owens observes, once the real differences of the philosophies have been removed, little if any philosophical consistence seems to remain. See his address, "Scholasticism—Then and Now," *Proceedings of the American Catholic Philosophical Association*, 40 (1966), p. 3, note. See also J. Collins, "The Problem of a Philosophia Perennis," *Thought*, 28 (1953), pp. 571-597; C. B. Schmitt, "Perennial Philosophy: from Agostino Steuco to Leibniz," *Journal of the History of Ideas*, 27 (1966), pp. 505-532.

40. Descartes, *Lettre à Mersenne;* ed. Adam-Tannery (Paris, 1897), I, pp. 151-152; *Lettre à Mesland*, IV, pp. 118-119; *Réponses aux 6es Objections*, VII, p. 436; IX, p. 236.

41. See Leibniz, *Theodicy*, n. 184; trans. E. M. Huggard (London: Routledge & K. Paul, 1952), p. 243.

42. See Leibniz, ibid.; Descartes, *Lettre à Mersenne*, I, p. 150. See Duns Scotus: ". . . si ponere per impossibile, quod Deus non esset, et quod tri-

angulus esset, adhuc habere tres angulos resol-
veretur ut in naturam trianguli." *Rep. Paris.,*
Prol., III, quaestiuncula 4; *Opera Omnia,* (Paris,
1894), 22, p. 53. See E. Gilson, *Jean Duns Scot*
(Paris: J. Vrin, 1952), p. 185, n. 2.

43. I am borrowing this phrase from Gilson, who
uses it to describe Avicenna's essences. See E.
Gilson, *Being and Some Philosophers,* 2nd ed.
(Toronto: Pontifical Institute of Mediaeval
Studies, 1952), p. 76. The phrase is not inap-
propriate because Avicenna's notion of essence
betrays the same essentialism underlying this
doctrine of eternal truths.

44. See Duns Scotus, *Ordinatio,* I, d. 3, p. 1, q. 4;
Opera Omnia (Vatican, 1954), III, p. 160, n.
262. The eternal truths are seen by the human
mind in the eternal ideas as in a proximate object. Ibid., p. 160, n. 261. See E. Gilson, *Jean
Duns Scot,* pp. 567-569.

45. ". . . igitur huiusmodi enuntiationes, quae di-
cuntur esse in primo, imo etiam quae sunt in
secundo modo dicendi per se, habent perpetuam
veritatem, non solum ut sunt in divino intellectu,
sed etiam secundum se, ac praescindendo ab
illo." Suarez, *Disputationes Metaphysicae,* d. 31,
s. 12, n. 40 (Paris, 1877), 26, p. 295.

46. "Est igitur valde communis ac recepta sententia,
has propositiones esse perpetuae veritatis . . . et
eam sequi videtur D. Thomas, citatis locis,
quamvis totam hanc perpetuitatem referat ad
intellectum divinum." Suarez, ibid., n. 41.

47. Ibid., n. 39, p. 294. For the difference between
the Thomist and Suarezian notions of eternal
truths, see P. Garin, *Thèses Cartésiennes et
Thèses Thomistes* (Paris: Desclée de Brouwer,

1931), p. 131. Speaking of Suarez' doctrine, he says: ". . . s'il y a encore un lien entre la pensée divine et les vérités éternelles, c'est à condition que ce lien laisse subsister une certaine indépendence de fond et une certaine autonomie de ces dernières."

48. *In I Sent.*, d. 19, q. 5, a. 1; ed. Mandonnet (Paris, 1929), I, p. 487.

49. See *In I Sent.*, d. 19, q. 5, a. 3, p. 495; *De Veritate,* q. 1, a. 5, p. 15; *Summa Theol.*, I, q. 16, a. 7. See A. Maurer, "St. Thomas and Eternal Truths," *Mediaeval Studies,* 32 (1970), pp. 91-107.

The eternity of truth has a different meaning for Heidegger. It will not be adequately proved that there are eternal truths, he writes, until someone has succeeded in demonstrating that Dasein has been and will be for all eternity. See *Being and Time,* I, 6, 227, p. 269. But for St. Thomas, even if human being (Dasein) had no beginning or end, it would still not be eternal in the proper sense. Its being would still be temporal and historical and so too its truth.

50. ". . . quia intellectus noster non est aeternus, nec veritas enuntiabilium quae a nobis formantur, est aeterna, sed quandoque incoepit." *Summa Theol.*, I, q. 16, a. 7, ad 4m. St. Thomas here replies to the objection that the truth of propositions is eternal, for granted that their truth had a beginning, it must eternally be true that truth did not exist before. St. Thomas retorts: "Before such truth existed, it was not true to say that such a truth did exist, except by reason of the divine intellect, wherein alone truth is eternal."

51. ". . . the truth of our intellect is a real truth, and one that is truly ours since we make it." E. Gil-

son, *The Spirit of Mediaeval Philosophy*, trans. A. H. C. Downes (New York: Scribner's, 1940), p. 267. "He (St. Thomas) is saying that we make the truth of our knowledge, not in the sense that what we make we can also unmake, *e.g.*, make the true (six is six) false (six is not six) or *vice versa*, but in the sense that unless *we* make it the knowledge will not be made, *i.e.*, *we* shall not have true knowledge." G. Smith, *Natural Theology. Metaphysics II* (New York: Macmillan, 1951), p. 44.

52. See *Summa Theol.*. I, q. 85, a. 4, ad 1m.

53. The spiritual operations of the soul have temporal succession but, unlike bodily movements, they do not have continuity. Some operations of the soul (e.g. imagination) have continuity *per accidens* owing to their relation to the body. See *In I Sent.*, d. 8, q. 3, a. 3, ad 4m, p. 216.

54. "Quia enim homo subiacet mutationi et tempori, in quo prius et posterius locum habent, successive cognoscit res, quaedam prius et quaedam posterius; et inde est quod praeterita memoramur, videmus praesentia et praenosticamur futura. Sed Deus, sicut liber est ab omni motu . . . ita omnem temporis successionem excedit, nec in eo invenitur praeteritum nec futurum, sed praesentialiter omnia futura et praeterita ei adsunt; sicut ipse Moysi famulo suo dicit 'Ego sum qui sum'." A. Dondaine, "La Lettre de saint Thomas à l'Abbé du Montcassin." *St. Thomas Aquinas 1274-1974. Commemorative Studies* (Toronto: Pontifical Institute of Mediaeval Studies, 1974), I, p. 108.

55. "Unde veritas divini intellectus est immutabilis. Veritas autem intellectus nostri mutabilis est."

Summa Theol., I, q. 16, a. 8. See A. Maurer, "St. Thomas and Changing Truths," *Atti del Congresso Internazionale. Tommaso d'Aquino nel suo Settimo Centenario*, 6 (Naples: Edizioni Domenicane Italiane, 1977), pp. 267-275

56. See *De Veritate*, q. 1, a. 6, p. 24.

57. Ibid., ad 4m.

58. Ibid., ad 6m, p. 25. Time plays a role in a proposition because it includes a verb, which signifies temporally. See *In I Periherm.*, lect. 4, n. 7; ed. Leonine (Rome, 1882), I, p. 20. See also *In I Sent.*, d. 8, q. 2, a. 3, p. 207.

59. "Unde patet quod nulla veritas est necessaria in creaturis." *In I Sent.*, d. 19, q. 5, a. 3, p. 496.

60. Ibid., ad 4m. p. 497. See G. B. Phelan, "Verum sequitur esse rerum," *Mediaeval Studies*, I (1939), pp. 11-22; reprinted in *G. B. Phelan, Selected Papers* (Toronto: Pontifical Institute of Mediaeval Studies, 1967), pp. 133-154.

"Now, our known conformity with the things understood, our truth, is not eternal; it began and ceases with our thought. It is not immutable, not that truth itself is subject to change, but our truth is subject to change; sometimes we are right, sometimes we are wrong. Nor is our truth necessary: it need not have been at all, much less need it have been necessarily. All these characteristics—eternity, necessity, immutability —are characteristics of the Truth which is God." G. Smith, *Natural Theology. Metaphysics II* (New York: Macmillan, 1951), p. 46, note.

61. ". . . veritas propositorum necessariorum potest deficere per accidens quantum ad esse quod habet in anima vel in rebus si res illae deficerent:

tunc enim non remanerent istae veritates nisi in Deo, in quo sunt una et eadem veritas." *In I Sent.*, d. 19, q. 5, a. 3, ad 7m, p. 498.

62. "Dicendum quod ratio circuli, et duo et tria esse quinque, habent aeternitatem in mente divina." *Summa Theol.*, I, q. 16, a. 7, ad 1m.

63. See A. Dempf, *Sacrum Imperium. Geschichts- und Staatsphilosophie des Mittelalters und der politischen Renaissance* (Darmstadt, 1954), pp. 367, 381, 397; *Christliche Philosophie* (Bonn, 1952), p. 134.

64. Quoted by M. Seckler, *Le Salut et l'Histoire. La Pensée de saint Thomas d'Aquin sur la Théologie de l'Histoire* (Paris: Editions du Cerf, 1967), p. 20. This remarkable book is a study of St. Thomas' conception of time and history in relation to the problem of salvation. It is a translation of *Das Heil in der Geschichte. Geschichts- theologisches Denken bei Thomas von Aquin* (Munich: Kösel, 1964).

65. Hegel, *Lectures on the History of Philosophy*, trans. E. S. Haldane and F. H. Simson (London: Routledge & K. Paul, 1898), III, p. 52.

66. See the work of Seckler, above, note 64. Also J. Langois, "Prémiers Jalons d'une Philosophie Thomiste de l'Histoire," *Revue des Sciences Ec- clésiastiques*, 14 (1962), pp. 264-291; M. D. Chenu, "Situation Humaine: Corporalité et Tem- poralité," 2nd ed. in *L'Evangile dans le Temps* (Paris: 1962), pp. 411-436.

67. *In I Ethic.*, lect. 11; ed. Leonine, I (Rome, 1969), p. 39. See Aristotle, *Nic. Ethics*, I, 7, 1098a23.

68. "Dicendum quod antiqui philosophi paulatim et quasi pedetentim intraverunt in cognitionem

veritatis." *Summa Theol.*, I, q. 44, a. 2. See *De
Potentia Dei*, q. 3, a. 5; q. 3, a. 17; *De Spirit-
ualibus Creaturis*, a. 5; *De Substantiis Separatis*,
1-10, ed. F. J. Lescoe (West Hartford, Connecti-
cut, 1962), pp. 35-98. In the sphere of practical
knowledge St. Thomas recognized not only pri-
mary moral principles common to all men and
true for all, but also secondary principles and
laws which change with time and the developing perfection and needs of man. See *Summa
Theol.*, I-II, q. 94, a. 4-5; q. 95, a. 1-2.

St. Thomas also recognized the temporal character of scientific hypotheses. He considered the
Ptolemaic system of astronomy to be an account
of the celestial phenomena observed in his own
day, but he envisaged a day when the phenomena might be "saved" in another way. See
In II De Caelo et Mundo, lect. 17, n. 2; ed.
Leonine (Rome, 1899), III, pp. 186-187; *Summa Theol.*, I, q. 32, a. 1, ad 2m. He tells us of
a man who spent thirty years investigating the
nature of the bee without knowing it perfectly.
In Symbolum Apostolorum, a. 1; *Opera Omnia*
(New York: Musurgia Press, 1950), 16, p. 135.

69. This is implied by St. Thomas in statements
such as the following: ". . . multa quae bene
sonant in lingua graeca, in latina fortassis bene
non sonant, propter quod eandem fidei veritatem
aliis verbis Latini confitentur et Graeci . . . Unde
ad officium boni translatoris pertinet ut ea quae
sunt catholicae fidei transferens servet senten-
tiam, mutet autem modum loquendi secundum
proprietatem linguae in quam transfert." *Contra
Errores Graecorum*, Prol. (Rome, 1967), 40,
p. A71.

70. *De Ente et Essentia*, 4; ed. Leonine (Rome, 1976), 43, pp. 375-6.

71. Considered absolutely, in abstraction from every mode of being (*esse*), rationality is predicable of man even though no man exists. See *Quodlibet VIII*, a. 1, ad 1m.

72. See *Summa Theol.*, I, q. 16, a. 7, ad 2m; *In I Sent.*, d. 19, q. 5, a. 3, ad 3m, p. 496; *De Veritate*, q. 1, a. 5, ad 14m, pp. 20-21. See A. Maurer, "St. Thomas and Eternal Truths," p. 100-102.

73. See E. Gilson, *Being and Some Philosophers*, pp. 76-88.

74. See above, note 37.

75. E. Fackenheim, "The Historicity and Transcendence of Philosophic Truth," p. 80.

76. See J. Owens, "The Primacy of the External in Thomistic Noetics," *Eglise et Théologie*, 5 (1974), pp. 189-205.

77. For Kant's Copernican revolution, see his *Critique of Pure Reason*, Preface to Second Edition, B xvi, trans. N. K. Smith (London: Macmillan, 1950), p. 22.

The Aquinas Lectures

Published by the Marquette University Press
Milwaukee, Wisconsin 53233
United States of America

#1 St. Thomas and the Life of Learning (1937)
by John F. McCormick, S.J. (1874-1943)
professor of philosophy, Loyola University.
ISBN 0-87462-101-1

#2 St. Thomas and the Gentiles (1938) by Morti-
mer J. Adler, Ph.D., Director of the Institute of Philosophical Research, San Francisco,
Calif.   ISBN 0-87462-102-X

#3 St. Thomas and the Greeks (1939) by Anton
C. Pegis, Ph.D., professor of philosophy,
Pontifical Institute of Mediaeval Studies,
Toronto.   ISBN 0-87462-103-8

#4 The Nature and Functions of Authority (1940)
by Yves Simon, Ph.D., (1903-1961) professor of philosophy of social thought, University of Chicago.   ISBN 0-87462-104-6

#5 St. Thomas and Analogy (1941) by Gerald B.
Phelan, Ph.D., (1892-1965) professor of phi-
losophy, St. Michael's College, Toronto.
ISBN 0-87462-105-4

#6 St. Thomas and the Problem of Evil (1942) by
Jacques Maritain, Ph.D., professor *emeritus*
of philosophy, Princeton University.
ISBN 0-87462-106-2

#7 Humanism and Theology (1943) by Werner Jaeger, Ph.D., Litt.D., (1888-1961) University professor, Harvard University.
ISBN 0-87462-107-0

#8 The Nature and Origins of Scientism (1944) by John Wellmuth, Chairman of the Department of Philosophy, Loyola University.
ISBN 0-87462-108-9

#9 Cicero in the Courtroom of St. Thomas Aquinas (1945) by E. K. Rand, Ph.D., Litt D., LL.D. (1871-1945) Pope professor of Latin, *emeritus,* Harvard University. ISBN 0-87462-109-7

#10 St. Thomas and Epistemology (1946) by Louis-Marie Regis, O.P., Th.L., Ph.D., director of the Albert the Great Institute of Mediaeval Studies, University of Montreal.
ISBN 0-87462-110-0

#11 St. Thomas and the Greek Moralists (1947, Spring) by Vernon J. Bourke, Ph.D., professor of philosophy, St. Louis University, St. Louis, Missouri. ISBN 0-87462-111-9

#12 History of Philosophy and Philosophical Education (1947, Fall) by Etienne Gilson of the *Académie français,* director of studies and professor of the history of Mediaeval philosophy, Pontifical Institute of Mediaeval Studies, Toronto. ISBN 0-87462-112-7

#13 The Natural Desire for God (1948) by William R. O'Connor, S.T.L., Ph.D., former professor of dogmatic theology, St. Joseph's Seminary, Dunwoodie, N.Y. ISBN 0-87462-113-5

#14 St. Thomas and the World State (1949) by Robert M. Hutchins, former Chancellor of the University of Chicago, president, of the Fund for the Republic. ISBN 0-87462-114-3

#15 Method in Metaphysics (1950) by Robert J. Henle, S.J., Ph.D., academic vice-president, St. Louis University, St. Louis, Missouri.
ISBN 0-87462-115-1

#16 Wisdom and Love in St. Thomas Aquinas (1951) by Etienne Gilson of the *Académie français*, director of studies and professor of the history of Mediaeval philosophy, Pontifical Institute of Mediaeval Studies, Toronto.
ISBN 0-87462-116-X

#17 The Good in Existential Metaphysics (1952) by Elizabeth G. Salmon, Ph.D., professor of philosophy in the graduate school, Fordham University.
ISBN 0-87462-117-8

#18 St. Thomas and the Object of Geometry (1953) by Vincent Edward Smith, Ph.D., director, Philosophy of Science Institute, St. John's University.
ISBN 0-87462-118-6

#19 Realism and Nominalism Revisited (1954) by Henry Veatch, Ph.D., professor and chairman of the department of philosophy, Northwestern University.
ISBN 0-87462-119-4

#20 Imprudence in St. Thomas Aquinas (1955) by Charles J. O'Neil, Ph.D., professor of philosophy, Villanova University.
ISBN 0-87462-120-8

#21 The Truth That Frees (1956) by Gerard Smith, S.J., Ph.D., professor of philosophy, Marquette University.
ISBN 0-87462-121-6

#22 St. Thomas and the Future of Metaphysics (1957) by Joseph Owens, C.Ss.R., Ph.D., professor of philosophy, Pontifical Institute of Mediaeval Studies, Toronto.
ISBN 0-87462-122-4

#23 Thomas and the Physics of 1958: A Confrontation (1958) by Henry Margenau, Ph.D., Eugene Higgins professor of physics and natural philosophy, Yale University.

ISBN 0-87462-123-2

#24 Metaphysics and Ideology (1959) by Wm. Oliver Martin, Ph.D., professor of philosophy, University of Rhode Island.

ISBN 0-87462-124-0

#25 Language, Truth and Poetry (1960) by Victor M. Hamm, Ph.D., professor of English, Marquette University. ISBN 0-87462-125-9

#26 Metaphysics and Historicity (1961) by Emil L. Fackenheim, Ph.D., professor of philosophy, University of Toronto.

ISBN 0-87462-126-7

#27 The Lure of Wisdom (1962) by James D. Collins, Ph.D., professor of philosophy, St. Louis University. ISBN 0-87462-127-5

#28 Religion and Art (1963) by Paul Weiss, Ph.D. Sterling professor of philosophy, Yale University. ISBN 0-87462-128-3

#29 St. Thomas and Philosophy (1964) by Anton C. Pegis, Ph.D., professor of philosophy, Pontifical Institute of Mediaeval Studies, Toronto. ISBN 0-87462-129-1

#30 The University in Process (1965) by John O. Riedl, Ph.D., dean of faculty, Queensboro Community College. ISBN 0-87462-130-5

#31 The Pragmatic Meaning of God (1966) by Robert O. Johann, associate professor of philosophy, Fordham University.

ISBN 0-87462-131-3

#32   Religion and Empiricism (1967) by John E. Smith, Ph.D., professor of philosophy, Yale University.   ISBN 0-87462-132-1

#33   The Subject (1968) by Bernard Lonergan, S.J., S.T.D., professor of dogmatic theory, Regis College, Ontario and Gregorian University, Rome.   ISBN 0-87462-133-X

#34   Beyond Trinity (1969) by Bernard J. Cooke, S.J., S.T.D., Marquette University.
     ISBN 0-87462-134-8

#35   Ideas and Concepts (1970) by Julius R. Weinberg, Ph.D., (1908-1971) Vilas Professor of Philosophy, University of Wisconsin.
     ISBN 0-87462-135-6

#36   Reason and Faith Revisited (1971) by Francis H. Parker, Ph.D., head of the philosophy department, Purdue University, Lafayette, Indiana.   ISBN 0-87462-136-4

#37   Psyche and Cerebrum (1972) by John N. Findlay, M.A. Oxon, Ph.D., Clark Professor of Moral Philosophy and Metaphysics, Yale University.   ISBN 0-87462-137-2

#38   The Problem of the Criterion (1973) by Roderick M. Chisholm, Ph.D., Andrew W. Mellon, Professor in the Humanities, Brown University.   ISBN 0-87462-138-0

#39   Man as Infinite Spirit (1974) by James H. Robb, Ph.D., professor of philosophy, Marquette University.   ISBN 0-87462-139-9

#40   Aquinas to Whitehead: Seven Centuries of Metaphysics of Religion (1976) by Charles E. Hartshorne, Ph.D., professor of philosophy, the University of Texas at Austin.
     ISBN 0-87462-141-0

#41 The Problem of Evil (1977) by Errol E. Harris,
      D.Litt., Distinguished Visiting Professor of
      Philosophy, Marquette University.
                              ISBN 0-87462-142-9

#42 The Catholic University and the Faith (1978)
      by Francis C. Wade, S.J., professor of phi-
      losophy, Marquette University.
                              ISBN 0-87462-143-7

#43 St. Thomas and Historicity (1979) by Armand
      Maurer, C.S.B., professor of philosophy, Uni-
      versity of Toronto and the Pontifical Institute
      of Mediaeval Studies, Toronto.
                              ISBN 0-87462-144-5

Uniform format, cover and binding.

Copies of this Aquinas Lecture and the others in the
series are obtainable from:

Marquette University Press
Marquette University
Milwaukee, Wisconsin 53233, U.S.A.